cats

from tigers to tabbies

cats

from tigers to tabbies

By Maria Mihalik Higgins

Illustrated by Anders Wenngren

PUBLISHING

Discovery Channel Publishing

Crown Publishers, Inc., New York

Published by Crown Publishers, Inc., a Random House company,
201 East 50th Street, New York, New York 10022

http://www.randomhouse.com/

CROWN is a trademark of Crown Publishers, Inc.

Printed in the United States of America

Library of Congress Cataloging-in-Publication Data
Higgins, Maria Mihalik.
Cats : from tigers to tabbies / by Maria Mihalik Higgins ;
illustrated by Anders Wenngren.
     p.   cm.
Includes index.
Summary: Presents information about the physical
characteristics and behavior of both wild and domestic cats.
1. Felidae—Juvenile literature. 2. Cats—Juvenile literature.
[1. Felidae. 2. Cats.] I. Wenngren, Anders, ill. II. Title.
QL737.C23C346   1998
599.75—dc21   97-43379

ISBN   0-517-80002-0 (paperback)
         0-517-80003-9 (lib. bdg.)

Inspired by Animal Planet, the cable television network from
the people who bring you the Discovery Channel. For more
information about Animal Planet's availability on your basic
channel line-up, contact your cable or satellite company and
visit our web site at *www.animal.discovery.com.*

For Emmaline, my own cub,
and David, who lets me roar.

Art Director: David Cullen Whitmore
Design: Studio A

All photographs supplied by Bruce
Coleman, Inc., except where otherwise
indicated.

Credits from left to right are
separated by semicolons, from top
to bottom by dashes.

Cover: Laura Riley—Peter Davy.
6, 7: Karl Ammann. 9: Kjell B. Sandved.
10:Kim Taylor. 13: John Shaw.
14,17: Erwin & Peggy Bauer.
18: Norman Myers. 21: Frank W. Lane.
23: Joe McDonald. 24, 27: Jane Burton.
28, 29: H. Reinhard. 31: H. Hartman.
33: Tom Brakefield. 34: Jane Burton.
38: Robert P. Carr. 41: Ed R. Degginger.
42: Karl Ammann. 44: W. Ostgathe.
47: Tom Brakefield. 49: Norman Owen
Tomalin. 50, 51: Doug Armand, Tony
Stone Images. 53: Larry Allan.
56: Jane Burton. 57: Fritz Prenzel,
Animals Animals; Robert Pearcy,
Animals Animals—Henry Ausloos,
Animals Animals; Gerard Lacz,
Animals Animals. 59: Giorgio
Nimatallah, Art Resource, NY.
60: Erich Lessing, Art Resource, NY.
61: Hulton Getty Picture Collection,
Tony Stone Images. 62: Erich Lessing,
Art Resource, NY. 63: Werner Forman
Archive, Art Resource, NY. Back cover:
W. Ostgathe.

Contents

cats: front

a sleek, unique physique

to back

Speed Racer

A cheetah gives hot pursuit to prey with the help of 22-foot-long strides performed at 70 miles an hour—a speed it can reach in only three seconds after a standing start. But while it may have speed, it doesn't have much endurance. A cheetah tires after running the length of about one and a half football fields.

Cat Scan

All Cats, Great and Small
Size and sound matter when classifying the family Felidae. There are seven "big cats"—the lion, tiger, cheetah, jaguar, leopard, snow leopard, and puma. Of these, four—the lion, tiger, jaguar, and leopard—can roar. None of the 30 species of domestic and small wild cats comes close to a roar.

Old-Age Homes
Big cats in the wild are lucky to live past 10 or 12 years. Those well cared for in a zoo can add as much as a decade to their lifespan, while cats kept in a circus may live even longer. The big top is such a great advantage, some experts think, because of the stimulation and exercise the performing animals receive.

Dem Bones, Dem Bones, Dem Cat Bones
A cat's skeleton has about 250 bones, 40 more than a human's. The longer the tail, the more bones the cat has.

▶ That's MISTER Tiger to You
Male tigers earn their stripes as the world's biggest felines. They typically weigh between 400 and 600 pounds, but some of them weigh in at a crushing 800 pounds—as much as two sumo wrestlers.

▼ Does the Tooth Fairy Leave Catnip?
Cats, like most mammals, get two sets of teeth. They usually swallow the first, or deciduous teeth. Their second, or permanent teeth, are in by the time cats are about seven months old.

Cat Scan

That's Quite a Shiner
Cats can see about six times better than humans at night, thanks to an extra layer of reflecting eye cells called a *tapetum lucidum*. These cells also give cats' eyes that weird glow when light hits them.

Caught Napping

From your lazy little house cat to the king of beasts, all cats take short naps whenever they can. They typically slumber for roughly 18 of every 24 hours. This means a nine-year-old feline has been awake for less than three years!

Counting Mice?

Cats, like people, experience rapid eye movement (REM)—a hallmark of dreaming—while they sleep. Although this doesn't prove they dream, it suggests they might.

Hid Lid

In addition to the upper and lower eyelid, cats have a third lid, called the haw. Tucked at the inner corner of the eye, this transparent flap moves sideways to spread tears, like a windshield wiper.

Meat-Seeking Missiles

Big cats can run fast but not far, so they must creep close to their prey before making a final sprint-and-pounce. Bolting prematurely would give the target enough time to escape. Because their eyes are on the front of their face rather than on the sides, cats can accurately judge how far away the next meal is lurking, and can perfectly time their attack.

▼ Ol' Grandcat

When a tabby named "Ma" died in 1957 at age 34, she had more than doubled the lifespan of the average house cat, who lives nine to 15 years.

Cat Scan

Laid-Back Cats

Domestic cats are more docile by nature than wild cats thanks to smaller adrenal glands, which produce the chemicals that make an animal feel scared, take flight, or fight back when danger threatens.

▼ Keeping an Eye on Things

Always on the lookout, a cat often sleeps with one eye partly open.

▶Too Close for Comfort

With expanding citrus groves and new housing developments squeezing Florida's panthers into smaller and smaller areas and polluting their environment to boot, the animals are mating with close relatives. This weakens their immune systems and makes them vulnerable to epidemics.

Cold Nose, Warm Heart

A healthy cat's nose is usually moist and cool. A dry, warm nose may be a sign of a sick kitty.

But I've Got a Date with Tom Tonight!

Cats can get blackheads and acne on their face and tail. The treatment is one familiar to every human teen: a mild, over-the-counter acne lotion with benzoyl peroxide.

Fixed for Life

Neutered males live an average of three years longer than unaltered toms. Not only do they get into fewer fights, they also seem better able to ward off infection.

▲ Don't Hunt Me Because I'm Beautiful

The Himalayan snow leopard has the thickest, softest fur of any feline. Such beauty has made it the most coveted big cat. Even international pelt embargoes are failing this alpine feline, whose numbers in the world have dwindled to fewer than a thousand.

CIA: Cat Intelligence Apparatus

Whiskers are as complex and sensitive as any radar device humans could ever invent. Embedded in bundles of nerves, these coarse hairs flicker at even tiny changes in air currents, and give the cat split-second intelligence about its environment.

Here a Hair, There a Hair...

In addition to the familiar twitching wisps on their snouts, cats also have whiskers under their chin, above their eyes, and on the back of their front legs.

Don't Leave Home Without Them

A cat without whiskers is, indeed, a sorry sight. Minus the navigational aid these hairs normally offer, a cat may misjudge distances and slam into objects, become wedged in a too-tight space, or even suffer eye damage from cruising through branches without closing its eyelids in time.

Fade to Black

All Siamese cats are born with creamy white fur. After a few months, the kittens' fur begins to darken into the "color points" on the face, paws, and tail for which Siamese are known.

▼ Mane Drawback

Lions leave all of the hunting to lionesses, and for good reason: Males' regal manes give them away on the open savanna and sabotage their stalking.

Big Hairy Deal

Hair Peace

The lion is actually much smaller than he appears. Take away that billowing mane (it's light as feathers, but good at cushioning an enemy's blows), and all you've got is...well, you've still got a 500-pound killing machine. But that mane makes him look even more intimidating to challengers to his territory, or even to females thinking of spurning his attentions.

Pretty Slick

The fur of the Turkish swimming cat is slightly greasy to make it more waterproof.

Advance Team

Most cats have an under coat of soft down hairs and an outer coat of longer, stiffer guard hairs. Guard hairs, like whiskers, are sensitive to touch. They give a cat extra help with navigation, letting it know, for example, that when the outer fur fits through that hole in the fence, the rest of its body will fit, too.

The Shadow Knows

The sleek black panther, a type of leopard, actually has spots. The markings show up only in bright sunlight, a rare treat in its dark rain forest home in India, Java, and Malaysia.

Hair Styles

Breeders have produced more than 60 distinct color and marking combinations beyond the familiar tabby (dark splotches on lighter background), tortoiseshell (red and black marks), and calico (red and black on white). Among the fancy cats:
• Smoke (light hairs with dark tips)
• Van (colored head and tail, all-white body)
• Sorrel (cinnamon color)
• Seal (dark brown)
• Magpie (black and white)
• Harlequin (half white, half colored)
• Peach (pink-tinged marks on pinkish cream background)

◀ And Over There's Dotty

The spots on a leopard's face make it almost as distinctive as a human's. Researchers can recognize the different cats they're studying just by their face "makeup," giving each one a special name.

All are dotted and similarly colored, so how do you tell the difference between the fur of a cheetah, a jaguar, and a leopard? Count the kinds of spots: Cheetahs have one solid kind. Leopards sport a trio of darker, bean-shaped marks around solid, caramel-colored inner spots. Jaguar rosettes feature tiny, dark dots within some of the lighter center spots.

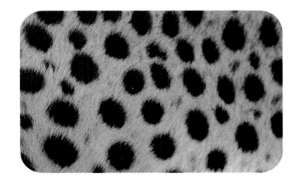

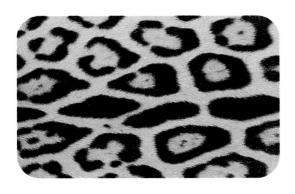

On Little Cat Feet

Putting Your Best Paw Forward

Most cats, like most humans, are right- or left-"handed." Roughly 40 percent are clearly right-pawed, and about 20 percent favor their left. The rest seem equally comfortable with either paw.

Getting a Leg Up

A cat always walks on tiptoe. The thin stretch of "leg" above the paw is really part of the foot. The pads on the bottom of its toes help muffle its steps as it sneaks up on prey.

Four on the Floor

There are five toes on a cat's front paws, yet it only leaves four toe prints. The fifth toe, called a dewclaw, functions something like a thumb and is located on the side of the paw so it doesn't touch the ground.

Fire and Ice

The 20-pound bearded North American lynx has paws as wide as a human adult's hand. These natural snowshoes come equipped with thick fur matting for cruising through deep drifts. At the other end of the thermometer, the Middle Eastern sand cat has extra-thick paw pads, and mats of hair between the toes, to protect it from burning rocks and sand.

Claws and Effect

Unlike every other cat's claws, the cheetah's remain visible when they're not in use. Although all of this speedy stalker's claws retract, they lack an outer sheath to cover them. This ready set of cleats gives the cheetah a head start when it tears off after prey.

Cat-Scratch Fever

A leopard's scratch is doubly dangerous. Its claws have deep grooves underneath that trap debris and germs. Even if the scratch is superficial, the infection could be deadly.

▼ Damage Claws

House cats fond of using the good chair or carpeting as a scratching post aren't trying to sharpen their claws—they're actually trying to shed the claws' outer layers to expose a healthy, new surface. So those little toenails that cat owners find on the furniture are no cause for concern.

Can-Do Cats

Monkey Bars

The tiny clouded leopard, found in Asian forests, and the margay, a South American wild cat, can turn a monkey's or squirrel's world upside down. They both have wide paws with super-flexible joints that let them scamper, facing skyward, along the underside of branches. They can even hang from one paw in pursuit of dinner. While other cats descend trees tailfirst, hugging the trunk, these acrobats can scamper down headfirst.

Work It, Cindy Clawford!

The cat has a notably sultry, fluid saunter. The secret lies in its loosely connected spinal column. Not surprisingly, a fashion show runway is called a "catwalk."

I Heard That

A cat's remarkable hearing, at its peak in youth, allows the animal to pinpoint the source of two different sounds less than two feet apart from 60 feet away. Each ear acts as a funnel and can swivel independently to catch sound waves better.

Hmm, Something's Fishy Here

The Asian fishing cat can swim underwater to grab a bite to eat. Its aquatic talent is helped by the cat's very own webbed feet, a feature found only on one other feline, the Turkish swimming cat.

▼ High-Wire Act

A cat's tail provides such good balance that the animal can stroll along ledges no wider than a tightrope without so much as a wobble.

▼ Low Profile

The ears of the Pallas' cat are positioned on the sides of its head. These cats scale sheer cliffs while hunting. If their ears were on top, potential prey could see the points sticking up over the rocks, giving the cat away before it could pounce.

Can-Do Cats

Humpty Dumpty Should've Had It
Several years ago a house cat cashed in at least eight of its nine lives when it survived a dive from the top of a 46-story building...with just a broken tooth to show for it. Cats often survive great falls thanks to their "righting reflex," a mid-air response that automatically flips the cat into perfect, feet-first landing posture.

No Place Like Home
Even if taken miles from home, many cats could find their way back. Some experts think the most likely explanation for this homing ability may be iron particles in their bodies that serve as built-in compasses.

Shout It Out
A lion's thunderous roar, which measures 114 decibels, can be heard five miles away. Standing next to one of these bellowing fellows would be harder on the ears than standing next to a subway train or sitting in the front row at a rock concert.

The No-Missing Lynx
Nothing escapes the attention of the small wild lynx. It can spot a mouse from 250 feet, or a hare hopping more than three football fields away. And its ears are equipped with antenna-like tufts of hair that help it capture the smallest muffled sounds in its forest home.

Bone Meal
With steel-trap jaws and rock-hard teeth, a lion can crack a bone in half with one powerful bite.

Leapin' Leopards
Balanced by a tail as long as its body, the snow leopard can bound 45 feet across a rocky chasm as easily as stepping over a mud puddle.

▶ Batter Up
The caracal, a relative of the lynx, is agile enough to knock a bird right out of the air. It will continue to fling any prey around until it is too injured to fight back. Only then does the cat go in for the killer bite.

Tongue Lashing

▼ If You Wanna Join 'em, Lick 'em

Licking the fur of another cat, called "allogrooming," is usually a cat's way of saying "I'm feeling friendly toward you"—not "You could use a bath; let me help you with that."

Lickety Split

The sandpaper-like roughness of a cat's tongue comes from thousands of hooklike projections, called "papillae," which help scrape every morsel of meat from a dinner bone. Big cats can draw blood from an animal's skin with just one lick. In gentle mode, their tongues clean dirt and blood from their fur.

Eau de Kitty

Face-cleaning does more than give a cat a tidy puss. With each trip the paw makes to the mouth to pick up saliva, it also picks up a scented fluid from glands in the chin. By rubbing this perfume into its foot pads, the cat then leaves its personal scent wherever it walks.

Good Scents

Of course a cat means no offense, but after people pet it, it licks off their scent and lays down saliva to restore its own.

Holy Hairball, Catman!

When a cat licks itself, it does more than spread its signature scent. The saliva kitty leaves on its fur also keeps it cool when it evaporates. And a clean, smooth coat is better at both holding in body heat during cold weather and keeping out moisture when it rains.

A Taste for Hunting

A cat's tongue is especially sensitive to the taste of meat—but it can't detect sweetness.

▼ Lick-2-3, Wipe-2-3, Lick-2-3...

When cats "autogroom," the scientific term for cleaning themselves, they always follow the same sequence: head and face first, with the side of a tongue-dampened paw. Next, they clean the front legs and shoulders, sides, and hind area, and end with the tail, cleaned from base to tip.

Sound Reasoning

Ready to Rumble

While there are as many theories about why a cat purrs as there are fleas on an alley cat, most researchers credit the sound to the cat's odd pair of second, or false, vocal cords. When contented, the cat quickly contracts muscles in its larynx as it breathes, tripping up the air as it passes through. The air vibrates these bony, nerve-filled structures, creating the sweet *"rrrrrr"* sound. The roaring cats have more flexible second vocal cords, which allow them to make such a mighty racket.

Chuffle Along Now

Here's a zookeeper's trick to try with the tigers: Imitate prusten, also called "chuffling," a signal that tigers and a few other cats use to show they're friendly. Snort softly like a horse through your nostrils with your lips slightly parted. The surprised cat may even chuffle back. In the wild, leopards and lions reassure each other not with prusten, but with puffing that sounds like stifled sneezes. Other cats show their goodwill with a watery gurgle.

Killer Cough

The leopard's mighty roar sounds more like a hoarse, rasping cough than like a call of the wild.

All-Purpose Purr

Cats purr not only when they are contented but when they are in pain or afraid.

▶ **Good Vibrations**

The rumble of a mother cat's purr calms her kittens—even before the newborns can hear. When her youngsters are nursing, they purr contentedly, letting her know that they are getting enough of her milk to satisfy them.

curious

why cats do what they do

Parental Guidance Suggested
Kittens grow up to be great hunters when their mothers show them how to capture and kill prey before the offspring are four weeks old. Their success rate nosedives without this well-timed training. Much of kittens' play is really practicing the hunting skills they learned at their mother's paw.

cats

What's Up with That, Pussycat?

Who Invited You?

When a cat buddies up to the one cat-hater in a roomful of people, it is simply singling out the least threatening human—the only one not offering to pet it or, even more important to Fluffy, not staring at it.

▼ Feline Forecaster

Cats have been known to predict volcanic eruptions, earthquakes, and electrical storms, running for cover minutes before disaster strikes. Experts aren't sure what makes cats such good forecasters. Some think they may be sensitive to the earth's tiniest vibrations, others think they feel the static electricity stirred up before a major natural disaster, while still others think that sudden shifts in the earth's magnetic fields may warn a cat of trouble ahead.

Roll Over, Beethoven

Rock 'n' roll, jazz, classical...countless cats have been said to groove to the beat of a particular kind of music. But a cat who reacts to music is really responding to a note or notes in the same pitch as one of its cat cries. In some cases, a cat's "enjoyment" may really be agitation.

Wacky Weed

That potent drug catnip will send half of the cats who smell it into a frenzy, while the other half will wonder what all the fuss is about. But cats have to be of age to play. Kittens younger than three months old will have no reaction to it at all.

Two tabbies, one jet-black, two all-whites, one gray: How can one litter have such a motley mix of kittens? A female cat may mate with several males, so the kittens probably had different fathers.

What's Up with That, Pussycat?

Love Is in the Air

That half-gag, half-grimace look a cat sometimes has when he's sniffing around means he's inhaling deeply to let air flow over an organ tucked in the roof of the mouth that helps him pick up even the faintest smells. All cats have one, as do many other carnivores. A variety of funky smells can trigger the reaction (called "flehmen"), but the usual cause in male cats is the scent of a nearby lady cat who's ready to mate.

Wrong Call

When a cat rubs, meows, and swats at the cord while its owner is alone and talking on the phone, it's not jealously calling for attention. Since no one else is around, the cat assumes its master is talking to it and comes over to be friendly. When another person is in the room, it simply assumes they are talking to each other and leaves them both to their people talk.

Spitting Mad

Most mammals have an inborn fear of snakes, which cats use to their advantage. Their hissing and spitting sound enough like a snake to make even large predators think twice.

▼ 0 to 60 in the Living Room

When Fluffy suddenly leaps up from a contented nap and zooms wild-eyed and puff-tailed across the room, up the curtains, over the couch, under the table, then nonchalantly settles again, as though nothing had happened, the culprit may be a lifelong hunting instinct that occasionally bursts through the everyday dullness, and that no cushy lifestyle of canned food and cuddling can ever erase.

▼ This Land Is My Land

A single tiger stakes out a territory as large as 250 square miles. No absentee landlord, it regularly surveys and marks—with urine, feces, and claw marks—points throughout the entire area to make its presence known.

The Tiger on Your Couch

You're Scent-sational!

They look comfortable, so why would a cat turn up its nose at one of those cozy little pet beds? Because it doesn't smell like its owner. An old, dirty sweatshirt draped inside makes such sleeping arrangements much more appealing. Cats like to snuggle on something with their owner's scent—the main reason, even above softness, that they like to commandeer beds and favorite armchairs.

Come Back Soon

Contrary to their reputation for being independent, domestic house cats like having their owner around. Experts say that the dug-up plants and other mayhem that sometimes greet returning owners aren't due to spite. More likely, cats engage in such mischief because they are anxious about being separated, or simply because they are bored.

Cover Up

Cats cover their feces in the litter box to hide their scent and show that they feel submissive, not to be neat. Outdoors, a dominant tom will leave his feces out on a high hill as a sign that he was there.

I Knead You

Eyes closed, motor running, drool dripping...and two clawed paws working its owner's lap like bread dough. This bizarre, trancelike ritual, called "milk treading," is mimicking the cat's action when it suckled its mother, treading on her belly to get the milk flowing.

Belly Up

Stirring from a nap, your cat stretches mightily and presents her tummy for you to rub. But the instant you do, you're rewarded with a swat and scowl. Consider the posture an honor. Domestic or wild, a cat's most vulnerable spot is its soft underside. By rolling over, your cat is really saying, "I like you, and trust you enough to drop my guard," rather than asking for a pet or tickle.

▼ What Goes Around, Comes Around

The cat wants in, the cat wants out. In, out, in, out. The feline isn't fickle, it's just periodically checking up on its territory. After taking a few sniffs for new smells and making a few deposits of scent, it's back to the couch for kitty.

Telling Tails

A cat wagging its tail isn't saying "I'm happy," it's telling you it's mighty upset and ready to attack. Cats' tails are emotion in motion. Here's a guide to reading some other signals a cat may be giving.

Calm, Relaxed

Submissive or Inferior

Aggressive, Ready to Charge

Adoring You

Mildly Annoyed

Very Afraid

In a Family Way

◄ Four-Season Fertility
Pumas can breed at any time of the year, a rarity among cats.

Bloodlines
Lions are the only cats that live together as a family. The group, called a "pride," may include many females, their cubs, and several males. The lionesses, who are all related, stay together for life. The few males, who come from other prides and are usually also related to each other, work together to patrol the pride's territory and guard their females from other males with mating on their minds.

Pride of Ownership
A male lion's hold on his pride is shaky. He will be challenged by new, often younger males who want his turf, and a fight— sometimes to the death—determines who leaves and who stays. If the pride's leader loses, he is cast out, doomed to roam alone or with some other male in a similar situation. Soon they will grow hungry without any lionesses to hunt for them.

Baby Boom
Take one pair of mating cats, fast-forward five years...and meet the more than 65,000 cats that have descended from the first two!

Get a Grip
The muscle-relaxing neck nip that a female uses to carry her kittens is a learned skill. New mothers may accidentally hurt or even drop their charges while they learn the proper technique.

▼ Maternity Loves Company
Many lionesses in a pride will come into heat together, and then will give birth together. Their cubs nurse from any of the mothers.

The Thrill of the Hunt

Pole Cat

A jaguar attracts fish to the surface by twitching its tail in the water like a fly fisherman's lure. Once a tasty morsel is in sight, the cat flips the fish out with its clawed front paws.

Family-Style Dinner

With teamwork and cunning befitting a military battalion, a pride of lionesses attacks prey with a can't-miss strategy. As they all move forward in a V-formation, those farthest left and right advance faster than those in the middle until they've formed a circle around a prey. When the center lion charges, the victim usually runs into the waiting group of cats ahead.

Catting Average

Quickly tired, the cheetah gives up on half its chases. Yet other big cats may be envious of that record. Solo lions lose four out of five hunts; tigers miss out on 19 of 20!

Sorry, Mickey

Birds appear on an outdoor cat's menu only infrequently. Rodents are its usual fare. It will only catch one bird for every 25 mice.

Still Waiting

A hunting cat can remain motionless for half an hour or more before charging surprised prey.

▼ Feather Wait

The ocelot, found in South American rain forests, will not take one bite from a captured bird until it has plucked every last feather.

▶ A Hunter Like No Other

The 40-pound African serval is tied with the cheetah as the most successful hunter. As most creative, it has no peer.

• To catch a tasty mole rat, it digs a small hole in the rat's tunnel. Knowing that the rat hates security breaches and will soon arrive to make repairs, the cat stands by, ready to fling the critter out with its long, curved toes.

• With huge ears that look like satellite dishes, the serval will sit quietly, its eyes closed, listening both above and below ground for the slightest scamper. Because even the faintest breeze will distort such delicate hearing, the cat cancels hunting trips in windy weather.

• Rather than risk losing prey in a chase, the serval will actually punch its victim to death in a bullet-fast ambush, typically as the foe is emerging from its burrow.

The Thrill of the Hunt

▲ Tall Order

Lions can take down giraffes, the seventh-largest land animals, even though they're 20 feet tall and weigh 3,000 pounds!

Fill 'er Up

For such a big cat, the 25-pound ocelot preys on rather puny fare—rats, mice, lizards, and other bitty critters. The hungry cat often needs to hunt for 12 or more hours each day to find enough food, a new mother even longer. This may be why ocelots bear just one kitten per litter.

Risky Business

In life-and-death duels, the winner isn't always the predator. A goring from an ox, a trampling by a buffalo, a swift kick from a zebra—even a pointed lesson from a porcupine's 30,000 quills—can kill a big cat.

Mighty Mite

The five-pound black-footed cat is so small that it spends the entire day in a hole hiding from predators in its arid South American home. And yet, at the tender age of 43 days, it is skilled enough to make its first kill. In contrast, tiger cubs are still fed by their mother at age two.

▼ Take-Out Meals

A cheetah was once seen sailing over a nine-foot fence while clutching a sheep in its jaws. And jaguars have been spotted dragging half-ton horses across rough country for more than a mile.

◀ There but for the Window Pane Go I...

When a cooped-up cat spying a bird outside tenses up and starts violently chattering its teeth, the cat is mimicking the killer bite it would use to slice into the bird's neck—if only that darned glass would disappear.

▼ Teacher's Pet

Those dead birds and rodents that cats proudly deliver to their owners' doorsteps probably aren't tokens of their esteem. Cats see humans as poor hunters who must be taught to fetch and kill food. Female cats, who are responsible for showing their young how to hunt, more often bear such gifts than males.

Food Fight

A cat "playing" with its prey before killing it is, in fact, dead serious. Most often the cat swatting, dropping, and recapturing the doomed critter is a spayed female who is acting out the maternal role she never got to play, bringing stunned but live quarry for her kittens to practice killing. In the wild, such "playing" can also be a matter of self-preservation. A predator must make sure its victim can't attack it before coming in close for the killing bite.

The Game of Cat and Mouse

Socks, twigs, paper wads, pens, and string in the paws of a house cat are mere stand-ins for the snakes, mice, and other unattainable prey it's pretending to hunt. In the wild, kittens and cubs spend months stalking leaves, mom's tail, and each other as they learn the hunting facts of life.

Hook Shot

That NBA-worthy, over-the-shoulder throw kitty performs at home with a wad of paper is mimicking the catch-and-toss instinct found in some felines who scoop fish from rivers and bat them onto shore.

Chowing Down

◄Caiman Got It

The six-foot-long jaguar happily includes the black caiman, the largest predator in South America, in its diet. A bold move, considering this cousin of the alligator and crocodile can grow to be 20 feet long.

I Could Stand Some Lunch

The desert-dwelling caracal is so comfortable being upright on two legs that sometimes, when eating, the 40-pound cat will stand like a human at a snack bar.

Binge Eaters

A single tiger can devour as much as 300 pounds of meat in just one day. At one sitting it can eat the equivalent of 300 hamburgers. Lions average 77 pounds of meat at a single meal.

▲ The Eyes Have It

The fishing cat's eyes can dart faster than any other cat's,
helping it follow the flitting fish it's stalking for dinner.
A researcher watched one of these water-happy cats trap
and eat nearly 30 frogs in three hours.

cool drink you just
p? Those purifying
er, not to mention
t left on the water bowl,
se cat about as good as
nd water would to a person.
urs later, after the chemicals in
ater have settled, kitty may lap it up.

Reserved Seating
Kittens and cubs immediately lay claim to one of their mother's teats, eliminating any turf battles.

Oh, Deer!
An adult panther eats 35 to 50 deer each year. Females with young to feed must nearly double their kills, bringing home the "bacon" about every five days.

Yes, That's How We Got That Expression
Although lionesses do most of the killing, males get "the lion's share" of a carcass before the females even take one bite.

Water Conservation
When a cat drinks, it curls its tongue like a spoon and flicks drops of water to the back of its mouth, where a puddle forms. It only swallows the water after several licks.

Zoo Food
Big cats in zoos are seldom given live prey to "hunt." Their typical zoo fare: preformed logs of ground-up horse meat and organs. They're served bony oxtails as crunchy treats about once a week.

▶ Chew on This

Lions and other cats rarely chew their food; they swallow whole bites at a time.

# of cats

cats' place in history

Catman

The ancient Egyptians' love of cats is legendary. The Sphinx at Giza, one of Egypt's most famous monuments, combines a lion's body with the head of Khafre, the king who ordered it built.

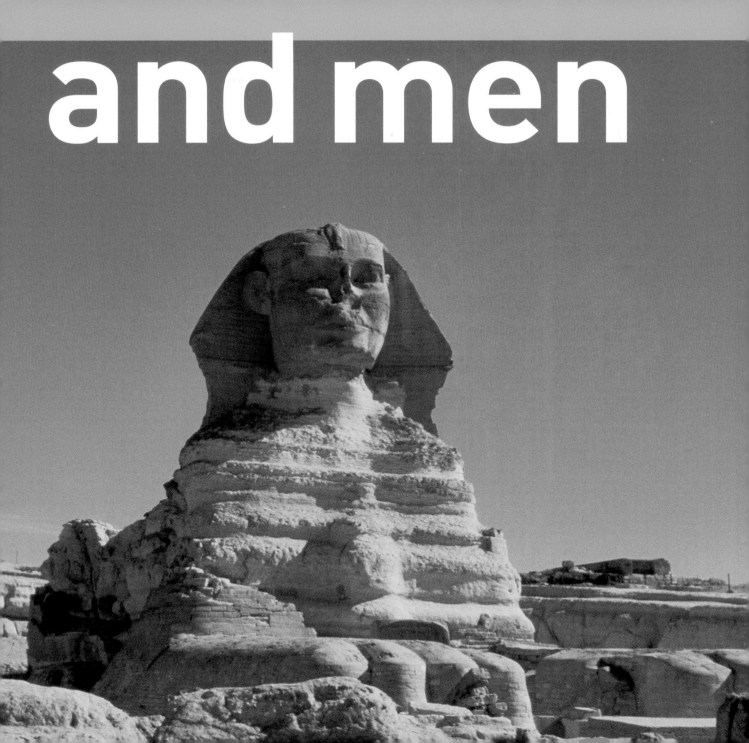

and men

Feared and Revered

Magic Cats

As with werewolves in other cultures, people in some parts of Asia believe in were-tigers, the name they gave to people who can turn themselves into the striped cat. In South America, Arawak Indians act out ceremonies in which men transform into were-jaguars to aid the powers of the local shaman, or spiritual guide.

The Cost of Kibble

Americans spend more than $2 billion a year—more than they spend on baby food—to feed their cats.

Doin' Feline Time

In one of the more unconventional programs at the federal prison in Lorton, Virginia, prisoners can adopt and care for stray cats, which brings a bit of peace and harmony to the lives of felons and felines alike.

The More, the Money-er

For every adult male lion living in Kenya, $515,000 flows into this African nation's coffers each year from tourists eager to see the king of beasts up close. Their value as an attraction has encouraged the government to enforce stiff penalties for poachers.

Tunnel of Love

In Florida, where fewer than 30 panthers survive in the wild, cars once kept hitting and killing the cats as they crossed a highway known as Alligator Alley. To help save them, people built a special 100-foot-long tunnel beneath the road, and now the cats cross safely in their search for food and new territory.

Got Them Coming and Going

In Bangladesh and India, locals working in fields and near the rivers have found a simple, nearly foolproof way to protect themselves from tiger attacks. They wear a mask with a painted-on face on the back of their heads. Tigers, who prefer to surprise their prey from behind, are tricked into believing they're being watched, and stay away.

Be Nice to That Cat

The Buddhist religion teaches that a cat's body is the temporary resting place for the souls of highly spiritual people.

Easily Rattled

It's common for cats in Paraguay to earn their keep (and their owners' gratitude) by hunting rattlesnakes, one of the fastest and smartest reptiles.

Reversal of Fortune

Black cats have almost always been linked with bad luck in America, but cross paths with one in Britain, and folks will envy the good luck said to be coming your way.

Feared and Revered

He Loves Me

When he wasn't writing his classic tales about Tom Sawyer and Huckleberry Finn, Mark Twain played billiards. So did his cats, who were allowed to roam on the table during games. Twain made up special rules for when they got in the way of the balls.

He Loves Me Not

In the early 1920s, one wealthy Chicago banker hated cats so much that he schemed to rid the world of them by 1925. He offered bounty hunters 10 cents for each of the first 100 they killed, and a $100 reward to the killer of the last feline on earth. Lucky for Fluffy, the deadline passed without success, and the man himself died soon afterward.

What Goes Out Must Come In

He's best known for his scientific theories about gravity ("What goes up must come down"), but countless cats should meow their thanks to Sir Isaac Newton for inventing the cat door, a flapping portal that gave his cat and her kittens freedom to come and go as they pleased.

Conquer That Cat

While Napoleon, emperor of France, was working in his tent one day, aides heard the general screaming for help and rushed inside. There they found Napoleon alone, his sword thrashing, claiming a cat was around. Nearly exhausted from the experience, he needed a doctor to help calm him.

Hail to the Cat

Long before Chelsea Clinton's black-and-white "Socks," Tad Lincoln gave America its first First Cat, "Tabby," when his father, Abraham, was elected president.

Explosive Talent

During World War II, British cats often alerted humans that Nazi bomb were on the way when the incoming planes' vibrations sent the animals darting for cover. One cat was even able to tell friendly Allied aircraft from German planes.

Frédéric Chopin, a gifted composer in the 1800s, wrote his famous "Cat Waltz" after his pet tripped across the piano keys while he was creating a new piece of music.

Kitty Catalog

In Your Face, Fido

Cats have run away with the title of Man's Best Friend in the United States. The country's 59 million house cats outnumber pet dogs by about six million.

Persian

Persians are the choice of nearly 80 percent of people who register their cats with the Cat Fanciers' Association, which has the largest cat registry in the world.

Pure White

Snow-white cats, which may be of any breed, often have blue eyes. But they pay a high price for their beauty: An inner-ear deformity associated with the blue-eye gene usually renders them deaf. Cats with one blue and one orange eye (a common oddity) will be deaf on the blue-eye side.

Maine Coon

The pedigreed American Maine coon is one of the largest domestic cats, often reaching 30 pounds—as much as a two-year-old toddler.

▼ Siamese

Owners take pains to keep their Siamese show cats placid. Prolonged anxiety or upset can raise the cat's body temperature, which changes its coloring. Heat actually can lighten darker points on the cat's coat, making it less attractive to judges.

▲ Scottish Fold

With squashed ears, this round-headed breed can't flatten back its ears to convey a foul mood the way other cats can.

▲ Manx

Without a tail, a Manx lacks the balancing finesse and communication aid the rear appendage provides most other cats.

▼ Sphynx

No shedder, this one. Except for a patch or two of thin fuzz, it's bald.

▼ American Curl

This cat's ears fold back on themselves within a few days of birth.

Classical Cats

How to Cheat at Hunting

For 5,000 years, cheetahs were captured and trained for royal hunts in Europe and the Middle East. When the hunters spotted prey, they whisked off the cloak they had thrown over the cat's head, and off shot the cat to certain victory. One prince kept 1,000 tamed cheetahs.

Cat-astrophe

In the Middle Ages, Europeans killed hundreds of thousands of cats. The rat population soared—and with it the flea population, which carried bubonic plague The disease swept through the continent, killing a quarter of the people.

Jewels of the Nile

In King Tut's time, pampered cats wore earrings.

▼Devil of a Time

From the Renaissance to the Colonial era, cats—particularly black cats—were believed to be witches' "familiars," their direct lines to the devil. Some kindhearted caretakers began breeding black cats to have at least one patch of white fur, and the "defect" often spared the persecuted puss's life. Their attempt was very successful. Pure black cats are still rare today.

▼ They Haven't Changed a Bit

Cats and dogs were popular household members in ancient Greece—although then, as now, they were not always popular with each other. So cherished were house cats that families shaved their eyebrows when a beloved pet died.

Classical Cats

▲ Cat Got Your Throne?
Pampered by maidens and priests under the orders of King Osorkon II, cats held court in elaborate Egyptian temples around 450 B.C. as cherished symbols of Bastet, the powerful cat goddess.

Circle of Life
Because a cat curls in a circle to sleep, ancient Egyptians believed it was linked to eternal life. The circle, like eternity, is never-ending.

***Mayflower* Meower**
Cats were common passengers on ships carrying colonists and traders to the New World. They earned their fare by keeping down the rat population onboard.

Cat Wrap
Ancient Egyptians mummified dead cats by the millions, often placing them in coffins painted with the cats' likenesses.

Fur Trade
China met its first lion in A.D. 87 when a Central Asian nobleman traded one for a Chinese princess he wished to marry. More of the cats arrived as Romans exchanged them for silk.

You Are My Sunshine
Ra, the ancient Egyptian sun god, was worshiped as a golden cat who brought daylight each morning by slaying Apophis, the god of darkness.

▲ Cat-apult

Persia overthrew Egypt in 525 B.C., thanks, in part, to cats. By setting scores of felines loose at the front of their ranks, the invaders effectively stopped the Egyptians, who would not fight back for fear of harming the animals they considered to be sacred.

Classical Cats

Get the Point?

With teeth the length of dinner knives, the sabertooth tiger struck fear into the hearts of men until only 10,000 years ago, when it became extinct.

Extinction Is the Pits

Among the more than two million fossils that have been recovered from Los Angeles' La Brea tar pits are the bones of more than a thousand sabertooth tigers.

The Mother of All House Cats

Wild felines moved from countryside to hearthside as early as 3500 B.C., when ancient Egyptian townsfolk began to realize that *Felis libyca*, the African wild cat, was keeping rodents out of their precious grain stores.

City Cat

Peruvian architects built the ancient town of Cuzco in the shape of a puma.

Going Against the Grain

In the tenth century, one Welsh king devised a unique punishment for anyone causing a cat's death. The wronged animal was hung by its tail, its nose touching the ground. The killer had to heap precious grain onto the body until it was buried—and then forfeit it all. The amount was meant to signify how much grain the cat could have saved from rodents.

▶ Hunting Cat?

Ancient Egyptians used cats when they went hunting to chase birds out of their hiding places in the weeds.

▼ Prehistoric Puss

In 34 million years, there are usually lots of changes in a species' family tree. The horse, for instance, ballooned from the size of a dog, traded its three toes for hooves, and grew a larger, longer skull. Yet, amazingly, the physical makeup of the cat family remains basically the same, as Stone Age art reveals.

Index